The ESG Data Revolution:
Sustainable Fuel for Tomorrow's Business

Michael A. Poisson

Published by MCMF Publishing

DISCLAIMER:

This book contains the opinions and ideas of the author. Careful attention has been paid to ensure the accuracy of the information, but the author cannot assume responsibility for the validity or consequences of its use. The material in this book is for informational purposes only. As each individual situation is unique, the author disclaims responsibility for any adverse effects that may result from the use or application of the information contained in this book. Any use of the information found in this book is the sole responsibility of the reader.

CONTENT

Part 1 - Welcome

Part 2 – Discovering ESG

Part 3 – The ESG Data Revolution

For Lucy, Lyle and Gabi

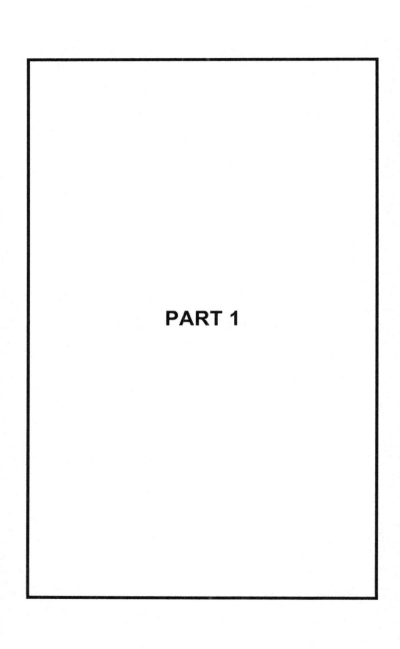

PART 1

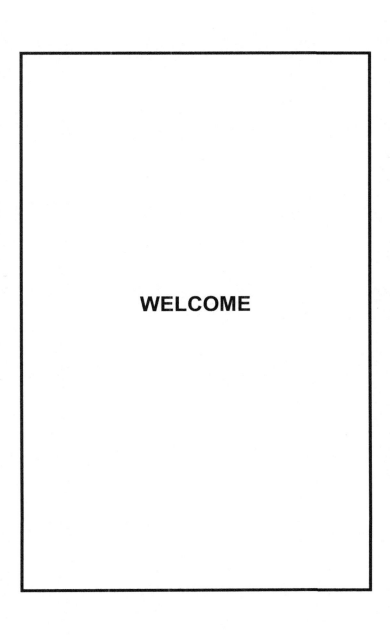

WELCOME

FOREWORD

Creative Construction:
ESG Data in Investment Management

The integration of Environmental, Social and Governance (ESG) factors into an investment process has become standard investment rigor among institutional investors. ESG data has been used to filter investable universes. ESG Ratings and ESG performance information about companies is used to test forecasting power of that information in order to generate Alpha, the investment return beyond a stated benchmark. Furthermore, beyond current financial materiality, ESG data is used for shareholder engagement, sector trend following, adoption rates of technologies, and therefore, the ESG research stands on its own.

Investors are sourcing ESG data in a variety of ways, from constructing ESG signals from raw company data themselves, using ESG Ratings data from third party vendors, to more recently using unstructured data, Natural Language Processing and Machine Learning to derive views of ESG issues.

Embedding E, S, and G information in the valuation process of a given security is a more direct approach, where one is connecting corporate activity (some E, S, or G behavior) to a line item in the financial statements. Since there are many debates about ESG data, its relationship to security market pricing and its role in fiduciary duty, Investors must be clear as to what the goal is in using this data given that at its core, ESG is not designed to measure the financial value of a company in a vacuum.

Questions arise when considering ESG data, such as:

- How and when to use ESG Vendor or Analyst Data, keeping in mind that ESG data alone does not make a "Sustainable Investment" make. These analyses are starting points to do further research on how companies are operating within their context.

- What does it mean that positive ESG performance is correlated with better financial performance? What does it mean that many large institutional investors are using this data now? It may mean that pricing may be more a reflection of greater demand for higher-rated companies based on the supply and demand for the stock from investors rather than from the fundamentals of the company.

- Can we develop algorithms to accurately assess the ESG performance of companies, sectors, countries? Do the ESG data vendors have it right? Are their signals predictive?

These and other questions ultimately serve an implicit use case of capital allocation that is purposeful and inclusive of the full value of a company and where ESG data has heretofore been regarded, incorrectly, as Extra-Financial Data, and in the milieu of Socially Responsible Investing (SRI). We are not just allocating capital for its own sake, but that capital is put to use for creative construction (Not "Destruction"). And while the purpose of a pension fund is to provide a pension off into the future, or an insurance company to pay its liabilities, achieving those financial goals must be built upon the effective allocation of capital into the economy that seeks to build the economy in the direction of sustainable development. And because sustainable development is humanity's only evolutionary stable strategy, sustainable alpha through creative construction is the only way to fulfill an investors fiduciary duty.

The ESG Data Revolution is helpful in answering many of the questions above. It provides a guide to the history of ESG data and how it has gone from a niche alternative data product to an industry in its own right. Michael Poisson also contributes a tremendous value to practitioners seeking to learn about the data by describing the business of ESG data and how it can help the financial services ecosystem.

January, 2023
Bruce M. Kahn, PhD
Senior Portfolio Manager, Shelton Sustainable Equity Fund
Faculty, Sustainability Management, Program, Columbia University

INTRODUCTION

In 2012, after decades of building, growing, and successfully exiting three FinTech companies, I found myself at a crossroads. We were in the process of selling my company, my mother was diagnosed with cancer, and I was soon to be without a job. After a very brief pity party, I understood that I was given a great gift, the gift of time to be with my mother in her final months. During this time, I found myself reflecting on both her life and my own. I realized that it was her commitment to service and social causes that had made her such a truly remarkable person in the world. And so, when a friend approached me about joining his business, a business that focused on researching and analyzing Corporate Social Responsibility and Environmental, Social, and Governance (ESG) issues, I knew what the next chapter in my life had to be. From that point forward, I was in the ESG Data Business.

Who This Book Is For?

I wrote this book to help those who are new to, or have never heard of, ESG and to engage experienced professionals in more dialogue and debate. It is designed to be useful for investors, entrepreneurs, and service providers who are actively creating ESG solutions. Venture capital and private equity investors who are interested in the growth of this rapidly expanding industry will also find valuable insights within these pages. Whether you're just starting out or already have experience in the ESG space, I hope you enjoy this book and let me know what you think.

What You Will Learn

The Amazon Bookstore tells us that there are over 6,000 titles available that refer to ESG. However, as of the day of publishing, this book is the only one that I know of that specifically addresses ESG Data and the businesses built around it.

The sheer amount of business that ESG data has created is mesmerizing. Countless businesses, from research and ratings firms to software and consulting companies, have come to rely on ESG data to bring their products and services to market. It has been reported that in 2021 the ESG Data and Products industry has surpassed revenues of $1Billion a year and is growing at a rate of 20% annually. The financial products created by ESG Data are growing by 35% per year.

In the pages ahead I will do my best to provide you with a basic understanding of ESG and ESG Data, where it comes from, and how it is used. And most importantly, the many businesses and business opportunities that are arising from this newly acknowledged field. This will include:

- A fundamental understanding of what ESG means and more specifically what ESG Data is.

- A look at the different approaches to how ESG Data is researched.

- An overview of how ESG Data is put to use.

- The multitude of products and services putting ESG Data to work every day.

- And, some thoughts, possibilities, and predictions for the ESG Data Industry moving forward.

This is not meant to be the definitive book on the topic but rather it is meant to be a conversation starter and an invitation to learn more about the subject and to consider your own contribution to the field. We need better ESG Data and we need more ESG Solutions.

So, if that sounds good to you, get comfortable, grab a highlighter, pen and paper, and get ready to join me for an enlightening journey. If you have any questions or comments, feel free to reach out to me at Michael@theesgdatarevolution.com. Thank you for your interest and enjoy the ride!

Michael

Chapter One

WHAT IS ESG?

ESG, or Environment, Social, and Governance, is a popular framework used by investment professionals to describe and analyze companies, countries, and even individuals with respect to their attitudes and impact on these key issues. By taking ESG factors into consideration, investors can gain a deeper understanding of the potential opportunities and risks associated with their investments, and make informed decisions that align with their values. This knowledge can help you make more strategic and impactful investment decisions, whether you're a seasoned professional or a new investor.

For three simple letters, ESG certainly causes a lot of confusion. This mostly happens because there are so many TLAs (three-letter acronyms) being used in the industry that represent very similar while specifically unique topics in what I'll call Responsibility and Sustainability. Let's take CSR and SRI. CSR, or Corporate Social Responsibility, refers to a company's efforts to make a positive impact on society. This can include reducing its carbon emissions, promoting diversity and inclusion in the workforce, and supporting sustainable practices. SRI, or Socially Responsible Investing, is an investment strategy that seeks to generate not only financial returns, but also positive social and environmental change. This can involve investing in companies that support renewable energy or sustainable practices, or in projects that promote social good.

For the purpose of this book, I will define ESG to be very specifically: **A lens to which one can observe a public or private entity's impact on Environmental, Social, and Governance issues**. It allows us to examine a company's performance on these important matters and can help guide investment decisions. ESG also supports something called **Impact investments**. Just to be clear, Impact Investments are those made with the intention to generate positive, measurable social and environmental impact (with or without a measurable financial return). Examples of impact investing include investing in affordable housing projects or microfinance initiatives in developing countries, in an attempt to use capital to generate positive changes in places of need.

The History of ESG: A Catalyst for Global Change

Many may be hearing a lot of talk about ESG for the very first time in today's news and social media, but it is not a new concept. ESG, as we know it today, is commonly believed to have begun with the awareness and consciousness of significant environmental, social and governance issues over the past 60 years. Some of the first major global social issues to gain widespread recognition was the age of apartheid in South Africa, when the Government practiced an oppressive system of segregation against their Non-White citizens. In response, the British government put pressure on the South African government to change its policies by boycotting South African businesses in 1959. The world was watching as international divestment of companies doing business in South Africa began in the 1960s. In 1977, the United Nations Security Council passed a resolution calling for a voluntary arms embargo against South Africa, and the Special Committee Against Apartheid was formed to encourage and oversee plans of action against the regime. Shareholder activism and resolutions against South Africa reached a peak in the 1980s, and finally, the age of apartheid was considered over in the 1990s.

The ESG lens shone a light on companies, countries, and individuals involved in supporting this social tragedy. Some might argue that the first ESG Data points were simply whether a company was doing business in South Africa, sourcing materials from companies operating in South Africa, or investing in companies involved in any way with South Africa. While ESG may have not single-handedly ended apartheid it did play a significant role in raising awareness of this social issue and empowering investors to vote with their investment dollars.

In the late 20th century, the dangers of tobacco became widely known. During this time, knowledge grew of the negative health consequences of tobacco. This coupled with the addictive nature of its business and the industry's targeting of vulnerable people from lower socio-economic backgrounds led to sickness, job loss, and even death. In response, values-driven investors took action by allocating their capital away from the tobacco industry once again relying on ESG research to find and identify the market participants.

Along with this social responsibility, awareness, and consciousness, faith-based investors were underwriting research focused on identifying companies, governments, and individuals involved in activities that went against their values. These "sin stocks" included industries such as guns, alcohol, tobacco, pornography, animal cruelty, animal testing, contraception, abortion, gambling, nuclear weapons, chemical and biological weapons, and cluster bombs. This marked a significant shift, as investors increasingly used their financial power to drive positive change and support companies and industries that aligned with their values.

The Importance of Each Letter in ESG

To describe the components of ESG at a very high level, it looks at how a company (a nation, an NGO, or an individual) treats the environment, its employees and communities, and its governance practices. In the environmental realm, the analysis regards points such as the company's use (or abuse) of water, its emissions of carbon, and its policies and practices on the use of plastic and recycling. The Social factor may include whether the company has a diversified workforce, creates jobs, has fair hiring practices, offers fair pay, and gives back to the community. And the Governance factor may look at whether senior management even considers social and environmental issues or how diverse (i.e. women, minorities, backgrounds) the board of directors is or if the Chairman of the Board and CEO are separate roles, whether the company provides proper training for its employees regarding anti-corruption and insider trading and whether executive compensation is tied to the management of these Environmental, Social and Governance issues.

As the 19th century progressed, Environmental research began to focus on wildlife habitat being dramatically reduced due to overhunting, deforestation, and wetland filling. In the 20th century, suburbanization and road building further fragmented and destroyed wild areas, leading to even greater concern. Today, environmental issues continue to plague our planet, from the destruction of natural habitats and the loss of biodiversity to climate change, pollution, waste, and the mistreatment of animals, and this is where the E in ESG plays such an important part.

Social issues have also grown to encompass a wide range of concerns, from diversity, equity, and inclusion, to employee engagement, wage equality, and human rights. Dealing with these issues is key for the well-being of individuals and communities, and addressing them is inevitable nowadays. ESG research has played a crucial role in bringing these issues to light and empowering investors to support companies and industries that are working to protect the environment, the people, and promoting sustainability.

"Without the 'G' in ESG, why bother?" This is how a friend of mine and a very popular money manager who is a popular speaker at ESG conferences starts every presentation. A prime example of poor governance is the Enron scandal, which occurred in the early 2000s. If you're not familiar with it, here's a brief overview: the Enron scandal was a series of events that resulted in the bankruptcy of the U.S. energy, commodities, and services company called Enron Corporation and the dissolution of Arthur

Andersen LLP, which had been one of the largest auditing and accounting companies in the world. The collapse of Enron, which held more than $60 billion in assets, involved one of the biggest bankruptcy filings in the history of the United States. The scandal sparked much discussion and led to new legislation aimed at improving accounting practices and standards. The Enron scandal pretty much embodies corporate board and management structures, as well as company policies, standards, information disclosures, auditing, and compliance issues.

The rise of ESG is undeniable. Nine out of ten publicly traded companies have adopted ESG practices, and for good reason: they offer numerous benefits, including reduced business risks, better financial performance, and higher returns on investment. And with ESG reporting mandates growing by 74% in the last four years, it's clear that ESG is here to stay. But we must not become complacent. There is still much work to be done to ensure that companies are truly ready for the ESG revolution. It's up to all of us to make sure that we continue pushing forward, driving progress, and creating a better future for everyone.

Chapter 2

WHAT IS ESG DATA?

As the world becomes increasingly aware of the importance of ESG factors, investors are gaining the tools and knowledge they need to allocate capital in line with their values. This evolution has sparked a surge in new products and services, helping companies to improve their ESG reporting and investors to better understand these complex issues. The ESG data and services market has exploded in recent years, surpassing $1 billion in 2021 and growing at a rate of 20% per year. This growth is a clear indication of the growing demand for ESG-focused investment opportunities and the need for better tools and services to support this important trend.

The Effectiveness of Quantitative and Qualitative Data.

I currently work for a seasoned and proven research and data vendor. We are constantly striving to provide our clients with the information they need to make informed decisions about their investments. Our team captures over 350 unique data points, including both quantitative and qualitative data, to assess companies on their environmental, social, and governance practices. As an example of quantitative data and how we operate with it, I will go back to our South African case example. If that were the case, we would ask the binary question of whether they are doing business with that country or not. Then, there's quantitative data that refers to their financial significance. Imagining that this particular company was doing a very small amount of business in that region and we learn through quantitative analysis that their exposure is *de minimis* (it isn't impactful enough) we may give them a pass on excluding them due to their business involvement.

Qualitative ESG data is a more subjective form of information that can be harder to measure and compare. For example, if a company doesn't volunteer their carbon emission output, we could attempt to measure the emissions by identifying how many times carbon appears through a scan of 10 million different publications on the web using artificial intelligence and natural language processing and building intelligent models. By analyzing the data, we can get a sense of its environmental impact. However, the world of ESG data is still evolving and there is an ongoing debate about which data points are the most important. Some people are going to invent what they feel is really important, while others are focusing on what regulators are looking for.

In order to better understand a company's environmental policies, it's important to ask questions about their approach to the matter. At first, a lot of simple binary questions are asked, for example: Do they have policies about recycling? Do they have policies about waste? Do they have policies about saving fuel, and things of that nature? However, more detailed information on their carbon emissions and other environmental impact is a quantitative exercise. That's where we get into what ESG data is.

Non-Financial Data and Its Newfound Power.

In recent years, European regulators have become increasingly interested in gaining a better understanding of companies' investments and operations. As a result, the data points that are used to assess these companies have become critical. One way that companies can provide valuable information about their environmental, social, and governance practices is through sustainability reports. These reports are voluntary publications that companies create and self-report, with no external oversight or verification of the numbers. However, despite these limitations, over 90% of Fortune 500 companies now issue sustainability reports. These reports offer investors and researchers insight into a company's operations and commitment to sustainability, allowing for greater transparency into their business practices.

We are used to looking at balance sheets and income statements. And we're used to looking at US GAAP generally accepted accounting principles. In the 80s when I started working, my first job was selling software for accountants and accounting companies. Everything I sold had to fit in something called FASB (Financial Accounting Standards Board). Back then, I thought that FASB had been around governing financial reports since the beginning of time. What I learned was that FASB was organized in the mid-70s to offer investors transparency into the finances of public companies. It was amazing to me that during the crash in the 20s, the average investor had no insight into the income statement and balance sheet of a public company. People bought stocks on insights, hearsay and advice. Therefore, FASB, a government entity, was created in the 70s, to offer everyone disclosure into the financials of public companies.

Today, there is an organization called the Sustainable Accounting Standards Board (SASB now a part of the IFRS Foundation) that provides a framework for companies to report their ESG data. Unlike the previously mentioned FASB, this is a non-governmental organization that was created by a group including Michael Bloomberg to provide a framework for reporting non-financial data. Based on an industry-by-industry approach, this data includes information about a company's carbon emissions, water usage, recycling practices, and diversity on the board of directors.

Non-financial data such as observations about trends and consumer preferences can be just as valuable as traditional financial information when it comes to making investment decisions. This was famously demonstrated by Peter Lynch, who worked for the highly successful Fidelity Magellan Fund in the 1980s. Lynch was known for his ability to pick winning stocks, and he credited part of his success to observing consumer behavior at the local shopping mall, including watching his teenage daughters go in and out of stores like the GAP. They were observations in terms of trends, and what's popular. In addition to the fundamental research that you do in the financials, you would add what's popular amongst the kids. It's now over 30 years forward and we're going back to Peter Lynch, and incorporating non-financial data into certain investment decisions as well as a number of every-day life decisions.

The importance of ESG and non-financial data is certainly affecting our decisions both consciously and subconsciously. If a company is considered to be run by "bad people" we may give them a bad G score. If the company is pumping a lot of carbon into the environment, may we give them a bad E score. If there are numerous complaints and accusations of bad treatment of employees, we give them a bad S score. To illustrate, I have an example from my own children. When my son arrived at college in Baltimore, shared ride services were becoming very popular. He was an active Uber rider until he read and heard of many allegations about how awful Uber was to their drivers and to people in general. The result was that he fired them! Voting with his dollars and choice of vendors. He hasn't been in the backseat of an Uber in at least five years.

It is clear that this non-financial information will play a critical role in shaping people's decisions about the companies, governments, and other organizations they support. While some of this data is reported directly by companies, other pieces of information must be gathered through research. Moreover, the impact of ESG data is not limited to large corporations like McDonald's and IBM. It is relevant to all types of public and private organizations and from municipalities and states to entire countries. As we move forward, it will be crucial for all of us to consider the environmental, social, and governance performance of the entities we support in order to make informed decisions that align with our values.

Chapter 3

WHERE DOES ESG DATA COME FROM?

As the world becomes increasingly aware of the importance of ESG issues, more and more companies are choosing to disclose information about their ESG activities. However, there is a lack of standardized disclosure requirements, meaning that each company may use a different template or methodology to report on its ESG efforts. This can make it difficult for researchers to accurately analyze and compare the data. While various reporting frameworks and standards have been developed in recent years, they are largely self-regulatory, allowing companies to choose their own method of disclosure. As a result, researchers of ESG data often have to rely on data that is volunteered, observed, or derived from external sources.

From Crisis to Responsibility: Self-Reported Data and its Origins.

The most common source of ESG Data is reported directly from corporations, governments, and individuals who have voluntarily disclosed them. This usually takes the form of a Sustainability Report. A sustainability report details the economic, environmental, and social impacts caused by the entity's everyday activities. – whether positive or negative. The sustainability report also presents the organization's values and governance model and demonstrates the link between its strategy and its commitment to a sustainable global economy.

The origins of sustainability reporting can be traced back to 1989 when the Exxon Valdez oil spill in Alaska sparked the creation of the nonprofit organization CERES (Coalition for Environmental Responsible Economics). In response to this environmental disaster, CERES released the Valdez Principles, a 10-point document on ethics, designed to guide corporations toward more sustainable practices and encourage transparency through environmental reporting. This marked the beginning of a movement towards a more responsible and sustainable way of doing business, with companies recognizing their role as stewards of the environment and agents of economic and social change. Since then, various international and national business organizations have developed their own guidelines for sustainability reporting, with the Global Reporting Initiative (GRI) playing a particularly instrumental role in the creation of the first global framework in 1999. Today, sustainability reporting is widespread, with over 13,000 companies adopting the GRI framework in 2019 and almost all of the top 100 US companies and 96% of the top 250 global companies providing some form of sustainability reporting, according to a 2022 KPMG survey.

Uncovering ESG Performance Through Observable Data

Despite the increasing popularity of ESG disclosure reporting, it is still quite common to find governments or individuals that do not provide consistent, measurable and comparable data. As there is yet no legal term that could help acquire such information, we may rely on observable data to gain insights into the organizations' performance data. Observable data is more frequently seen through serious journalists and bloggers who have been leading the charge in uncovering and disseminating information about an organization's ESG practices, particularly when those practices are not transparently reported. ESG-related stories are frequently covered by major financial publications such as The New York Times, The Financial Times, and The Wall Street Journal, as well as numerous blogs and newsletters. They recognize that poor ESG performance can have negative impacts on the environment, society, and a company's reputation, potentially impacting its financial performance.

In addition to these high-profile printed publications, there is also audio-visual valuable information that can be gathered about a company, government, or individual's ESG Data. We can listen to corporate earnings calls, attend annual meetings, monitor corporate resolutions, and read letters to the shareholders. And, of course, there is the never-ending supply of cable news executive interviews and an explosion of podcasts.

Going deeper into the multimedia world, as marketing becomes more and more important to companies to survive in our hyper-connected society, advertisement activities also became a target to observe ESG behavior. As examples of campaigns that could be used to make ESG observations, I refer to Coca-Cola's recent campaign to promote their first 100% plant-based plastic bottles. In the automotive industry, Ford is supporting carbon neutrality and pay equity. After being in even more evidence post-pandemic, Pfizer is highlighting the importance of access to healthcare in their company. And it has already been a while since Starbucks embraced diversity and inclusion in their company.

Observed ESG data can often be unstructured and filtered through marketing or PR lenses, making it difficult to accurately assess an organization's environmental, social, and governance performance. To overcome this challenge, researchers and analysts are turning to scientific approaches and powerful technological tools such as artificial intelligence (AI) and natural language processing (NLP) to collect, analyze, and understand this data.

The combination of AI and NLP allows for the efficient collection and analysis of large amounts of data, providing valuable insights into an organization's ESG risks and opportunities. For example, at a recent symposium offered by the Yale Initiative on Sustainable Finance, a research paper was presented on the use of AI and NLP to analyze the words spoken by a company's leadership during quarterly earnings calls, specifically they were observing positive or negative intonations in these words to assess the company's impact on environmental issues. This use of AI highlights the potential of these tools to provide more structured and efficient evaluations of high-yield universes, using the materiality framework developed to prioritize the most significant ESG issues for an organization.

Derived ESG Data: A Solution For Assessing ESG Performance

In cases where a company refuses to disclose any information about its ESG activities, it can be challenging to assess its performance in these areas. In such cases, one strategy that can be used is to perform a peer group analysis, which involves comparing the company to similar organizations in the same industry or location. This can help to make estimates about the company's ESG performance based on the practices of its peers.

Derived ESG data is becoming even more prevalent as a result of regulatory bodies requiring specific disclosures of metrics that aren't volunteered. This requires combining data from multiple sources and can be challenging, as different sources may have different update frequencies and methods of recording information. For example, calculating an organization's "CO_2 emissions per employee" requires data on emissions as well as human resources, which may be sourced from different systems with varying levels of data quality.

In summary, the sources of ESG data can include self-reported, observed, and derived data. It is important to understand the unique characteristics and challenges of each source in order to effectively collect and analyze accurate and reliable information. By using various strategies and technologies, such as AI and NLP, we can overcome the limitations of each source and gain a comprehensive understanding of an organization's environmental, social, and governance performance. As the demand for transparency and sustainability continues to grow, it is crucial to continue to develop and refine methods for collecting and analyzing ESG data to ensure that stakeholders have the information they need to make informed decisions.

A Real-World Illustration

IdealRatings®

Topic: The Business of ESG Data
To: Mike Poisson
From: Ghada Essam, Head of Strategy, IdealRatings Inc.

In 2006, IdealRatings, Inc. was established with the mission to empower investors and businesses striving to have a positive impact on the world. Since then, IdealRatings, Inc. has become a world-class provider of Responsible Investing and Sustainability

Solutions. We believe in the synergy brought by blending technology with top-notch research, and our mastery of that has pushed us ahead of the curve.

IdealRatings had foreseen the shift in investment appetite, from absolute returns to impact investing, and with our extensive experience in ethical investing solutions, we were able to design and create proprietary research methodology with vast granularity and neutrality, and arrive to market very early on, with an ESG data solution that provides both holistic and sophisticated, 360 degrees assessments of global issuers' sustainability performance.

But the road to nirvana was narrow and unpaved! The ESG data industry had and still has so many challenges to be addressed. To name just a few: Reporting inconsistency, lack of standardization, and areas of subjective assessments. Such challenges did indeed affect data aggregation and the ability of Rating providers to provide consistent data and ratings that are comparable across issuers and sectors. We worked for years to mitigate persistent challenges innovatively.

To address all of the static out there, IdealRatings created advanced internal estimation models, proxies, and AI tools to estimate as accurately as possible nonreported data, so that data can be normalized across issuers and sectors. The multi-layer estimation model includes various criteria upon which an estimation is executed. These criteria include the nation, business activities, and market size. Another challenge was normalizing ESG scores and ratings for corporations across different sectors and industries. For that, IdealRatings has designed a proprietary Materiality matrix by which investors are able to identify and prioritize ESG issues pertaining to their ESG Strategy.

Last but not least: Scalability. As the industry gained momentum and evolution of thought has become very fast, major challenges emerged in the number of data fields and number of companies to cover. And this is where we had to utilize AI and machine learning tools to assist in screening vast amounts of unstructured data and convert it to structured data that is preliminary and necessary for manual research to derive insights, data, and conclusions.

In setting our go-to-market strategy, we identified the challenges and the pain points, and hence, adopted a unique strategy by offering:

- Transparent research and scoring methodologies shared with clients.

- The largest, unrivaled investable universe that consists of 40,000 issuers, 450K+ fixed income, and 850+ REITs.

- High Granularity of data (350+) allowing for more focused attribution analysis and investment decisions

- Friendly Redistribution Rights: that accommodate various use cases for data sharing and redistribution.

- Customizable Guidelines: our backend tools were built to accommodate full customization.

- Thematic Mix: Applying different investment philosophies with screening processes that include: ESG inclusion, Norms-based Screening, and Positive Screening.

We have been preparing our clients for the day when sustainable investing and disclosures become mandatory, and that day has certainly arrived. We are committed to continuing to innovate and develop solutions that allow for investment decisions that are better for our planet and for the people.

Ghada Essam, Head of Strategy, IdealRatings Inc.

Chapter 4

WHAT TO DO WITH ESG DATA?

With the increasing importance of ESG issues, it's natural to wonder what can be done with the data gathered on these topics. Currently, there are over 150 companies that offer some level of research into ESG data and risk factors for companies, governments, NGOs, and individuals. While some of these companies offer comprehensive data on a wide range of ESG metrics, others may specialize in a specific area such as carbon emissions, water abuses, or diversity. Some may offer hundreds of individual data observations going back for decades while others may offer a single observation for a single company at a single point in time. The lack of a universally accepted source of ESG data can make it difficult to navigate this landscape, but the applications for ESG data are rapidly growing and evolving.

ESG Data in Action: The Use of Exclusionary and Positive Screens

One of the earliest uses of ESG data was to identify companies to avoid doing business with, using exclusionary screens. For example, some investors might choose to exclude companies that were involved in South Africa during the apartheid era, or that produced certain controversial products like tobacco or guns. These exclusionary screens could be driven by personal or ethical concerns and could be highly specific. In addition to negative screens, there are also "positive screens," which identify companies working on clean energy, electric vehicles or companies that are considered socially responsible based on factors such as job creation, diversity in the workforce, and representation of women on the board of directors.

These screens are helpful to determine who you may want to include or exclude in your investments or business considerations. But once the screening was done, how do you compare the resulting universe? Large research companies were soon to offer their own rating and scoring assessments commonly based on their own (and at many times) proprietary methodologies. The result was a numeric (generally 1-100) score and letter grade similar to bond ratings (Triple A to Single D) that represented each of the Environmental, Social, and Governance factors as well as an overall ESG rating and score.

The good news was that we now had a convenient way of measuring sustainability. However, these ESG ratings and scores created as much controversy as they did convenience. Many were quick to point out that you can't compare a bank to a mining company when it comes to environmental issues or maybe a clothing manufacturer to an accounting firm when it comes to child labor issues. Addressing these concerns, "frameworks" such as the Sustainable Accounting Standards Board (SASB) were created to debate these topics and offer solutions that include "materiality" into the equation. By asking the questions about what sustainability issues are people most interested in, they broke the world into 26 general sustainability issues. They then looked at the specific impact that these issues had on companies in specific industries. The result was a thorough consideration of how these 26 issues manifested across 77 specific industries and the development of their Materiality Map. Many ratings providers now offer a rating and score based on the SASB Materiality Mapping in addition to their own proprietary methodologies.

Evolving ESG Data Into Financial Services and Products

As ratings and scores became more accepted as a way to assess an individual entity, they were soon used to describe the entire socially responsible industry and all of its nuances. In 1990, MSCI launched which is considered to be the first ESG index - The MSCI KLD 400 Index which was designed to help socially conscious investors weigh social and environmental factors in their investment choices. And since then, thousands of indexes, index funds, Exchange Traded Funds (ETFs), and mutual funds can be found representing high green, low carbon, environmentally friendly, employee diverse or even negatively screened investment options.

Whereas these index products and funds generally represent collections of securities that satisfy a particular investment conscience whole new breed of investible products have been created which serve an ESG purpose of both the issuer of the security and the investors of the securities. Green, Sustainable, and Socially Responsible Bonds are examples of this. And, even more derivative and alternative investment products have arrived which will be discussed further in the next chapter: The Business of ESG Data.

With the evolution of ESG Data into financial (investable) products came the need for services to offer, implement, and manage these products. At one end you had the Investment advisors who would rely on ESG data, the quality of research, the applicability of the framework and who could deliver an investable product to their clients to achieve double-bottom line results meaning a financial return that has with it some positive effect on the environment, society or world at large. On the other end of the ESG data chain are the originators of the ESG data: the companies, governments, NGOs, and individuals who are being researched, rated, and evaluated. A variety of services have been created in order to support their accurate measurement formatting and reporting of their own information to ensure that the researchers and evaluators are doing their jobs properly. All the way down to measuring devices sitting atop smokestacks measuring the amount of carbon being released into the air.

Advocacy and Proxy Voting with their shares

ESG data has contributed greatly to inform shareholders on the companies that they are or choose to invest in. And since Proxy voting is the primary means for shareholders to communicate their views about a company's management, ESG data has empowered them to vote annually to elect board members and approve executive compensation packages and other strategic proposals put forward by the company and introduce their own resolutions supporting sustainability and other environmental and social issues affecting the company.

Navigating the world of ESG regulations

In the past five years, the push for ESG regulation has gained momentum worldwide. The European Union, for example, has made ambitious commitments under its Green New Deal, including a goal of achieving climate neutrality by 2050. Meanwhile, in the United States, the Securities and Exchange Commission (SEC) has proposed new requirements for public companies to disclose climate-related information in their public filings. One such proposal, known as the "issuer rule," would require companies to provide data on climate-related financial risks and greenhouse gas emissions.

Other regulations that have been introduced or are under consideration include the Sustainable Finance Disclosure Regulation (SFDR) in Europe, which aims to improve transparency in the sustainable investment market and prevent *greenwashing* (which I will discuss a little later in this book), and the EU Taxonomy, which sets minimum criteria for environmentally sustainable economic activities. Even ESG data providers are under consideration to regulate. Overall, these efforts are intended to increase transparency and accountability in the ESG space and ensure that investors and businesses have accurate and reliable information to make informed decisions. The uses of ESG data are forever evolving and expanding. The next chapter discusses the business and opportunities that have resulted from this.

A Real-World Illustration

YvesBlue

Topic: The Business of ESG Data
To: Mike Poisson
Fm: David E. Silver – CEO YvesBlue

Questions

- *What was the problem you saw?*
- *What was the solution that YvesBlue came up with?*
- *How is this going to change the Business of ESG data moving forward?*

The Problem – *Transforming ESG data into actionable insight/knowledge*

Having been involved in ESG for over 6 years, I am well aware that no single data provider has been able to deliver the comprehensive view necessary to leverage ESG/Sustainability factors for financial decision-making. Whether leveraging ESG for risk assessment or investment opportunities, today's data landscape is highly fragmented and incomplete. As a result, many financial institutions struggle with transforming multiple disparate data sets from multiple vendors to deliver clear and digestible insight in order to make sound financial decisions associated with ESG factors. These varied datasets include information such as company-reported information, specific carbon metrics, external stakeholder information, and many other sources of relevant content.

In order to deliver a holistic understanding of a company or portfolio, from a sustainability perspective, taming these varied datasets and transforming them into a single view has become a costly endeavor. These multi-vendor datasets were never meant to be combined with one another and created many unforeseen issues such as differing update frequencies, lack of common formats, and lack of standards in the industry to connect these data sets together, just to name a few. The above issues have created a significant challenge for many financial institutions looking to integrate ESG. As a result, financial institutions have been relegated to spending millions of dollars and multiple years in order to provide a trustworthy set of information for using ESG factors in making investment decisions.

The Solution – *YvesBlue's ESG as a Service Platform*

After leaving Factset's ESG division, I met with Anna Marie Wascher and the YvesBlue team. YvesBlue has been focused on solving the problem of transforming disparate data into actionable insight across multiple investment workflows. YvesBlue has achieved this by integrating over 25 data sources and delivering a cloud-based solution that mirrors what organizations have been doing internally by building in-house custom data lakes. Instead of spending millions of dollars and multiple years, YvesBlue is able to achieve the same goal of these internally built systems and get clients up and running in minutes rather than years, and at a significant fraction of the costs required to implement similar in-house solutions. YvesBlue's solution supports the ability to leverage this insight across multiple investment workflows including reporting, portfolio analysis and construction, engagement & stewardship, regulatory reporting, carbon attribution, risk assessments etc..... By providing a comprehensive platform this insight can be leveraged immediately or customized the way scores and insight are created to align to any ESG / Sustainability desired mandates.

The Impact – Delivering all of the necessary tools and expertise to help financial institutions accelerate the integration of ESG/Sustainability relevant insight to make investment decisions helping to mitigate risk, delivering required regulatory reporting, and assessing portfolio performance and attribution.

Rather than just focusing on delivering data, YvesBlue provides a comprehensive platform for creating and distributing the necessary insight to compete effectively for the purpose of monies flowing into ESG/Sustainability investing. YvesBlue provides this capability without incurring the time, expense, and expertise needed to attract and service monies that are directed for the purpose of sustainable investments. YvesBlue has focused on delivering actionable insight from data and delivers the next generation of data providers focused on the transformation of data into insight rather than focused on the collection of the raw data itself. It is putting the data into context that is important rather than focusing solely on the data itself. Only YvesBlue delivers a cloud-based solution that is helping organizations successfully integrate ESG across all investment workflows as well as access risk factors associated with their investments using sustainability as a factor. YvesBlue's solution is an extensible and customizable platform that provides for aligning ESG and Sustainability factors to clients and investment policy statements rather than a one-size-fits-all approach to ESG integration.

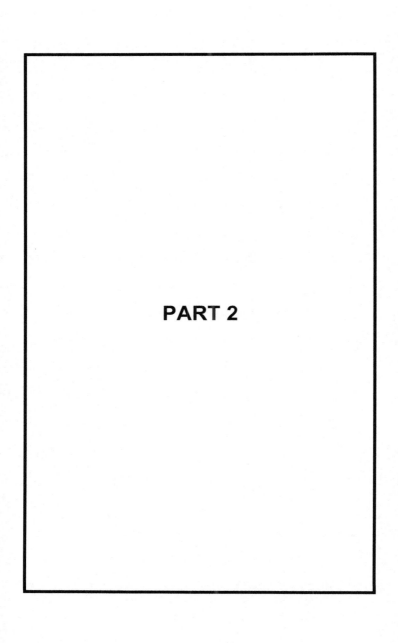

PART 2

THE BUSINESS
OF ESG DATA

Chapter 5

THE BUSINESS OF ESG DATA

The primary reason I decided to write this book was to highlight the many business opportunities that have become available with the evolution of ESG Data. Nowadays, there are hundreds of businesses serving the ESG and responsible investing market. The range is wide, going from negative screening to researching ESG risk factors to the creation of new financial products and software and services. In fact, by 2025, it is projected that the number of businesses related to ESG data will surpass one thousand. This chapter delves into the exciting and rapidly evolving world of ESG-focused businesses, highlighting some of the most innovative and impactful players in the field.

Dominating the ESG Data Industry: The Research Firms

There are over 150 research firms supporting the business of Socially Responsible Investing, each with its own unique approach, scope, and size. The largest and most recognizable research firms include MSCI, Thomson Reuters, S&P, and Sustainalytics (owned by Morningstar). These big research and data companies dominate the market share and currently account for more than 60% of the $1 billion ESG Data industry. Mid-sized firms such as (the company I work for) Investor Analytics, RepRisk, Arabesque and CSRHub may not have the same name recognition as the larger vendors, however, these mid-sized vendors have differentiated themselves on quality and scope of coverage, unique research methodologies, and other factors such as "consensus" services. And, a new generation of startups is emerging, such as Clarity.AI, Yves Blue, OWL ESG, and GaiaLens, which are making their mark with advanced insights and analytics, regulatory reporting, and cutting-edge AI and natural language processing models.

Many of the world's major stock exchanges and large custody banks are now offering ESG research and data either through collaboration, acquisition, or through their own direct research initiatives. An example of this effort to create "green exchanges" in the stock market is the Luxembourg Green Exchange (LGX) which lists companies that meet a minimum threshold of ESG performance.

As the amount of research on environmental, social, and governance (ESG) issues grows, more ways to access this information are becoming available. In addition to buying data directly from research companies, there are now many online marketplaces that redistribute ESG data. One good example is Factset, a company that has built a business model redistributing financial data from top providers since 1978. Recently, they acquired TrueValueLabs, a pioneer in AI-based ESG Data research, and after such acquisition, they are now a significant source of ESG Data. Other companies like Amazon and Snowflake also offer ESG data through their online marketplaces. Even big banks like JP Morgan and BNY Mellon are getting in on the game, with plans to offer ESG data through their own marketplaces.

Navigating the World of ESG Rating and Scoring Systems

With an abundance of data available from so many researchers and distributors, access to data is no longer a problem. But using the data to effectively compare companies, governments, and individuals can be a challenge. To help with this issue, there are companies working as raters and scorers. They offer numeric scores and letter ratings in ESG both individually and in combined performance. However, a major problem with this approach is that, unlike bond ratings which are determined by just three major agencies (S&P, Moody's, and Fitch), there are now an overwhelming number of rating and scoring systems to choose from, as many as the number of research and data providers.

The main reason for the many different ESG rating and scoring systems is that there is no standard way to calculate them. Organizations such as GRI (The Global Reporting Initiative) and SASB (The Sustainable Accounting Standards Board) have developed frameworks and guidelines to help understand what data is important for sustainability reporting and how to evaluate it. However, not all rating and scoring companies use these frameworks. It has become more common for companies to use their own methods, assumptions, and weightings to create their own "proprietary" rating or score. Some users of ESG ratings and scores prefer the "black box" approach and trust the big vendors' experience and expertise. But others believe that it is important to understand how the score was created and what the underlying methodology and data are.

A Look at the Key Players in Sustainability Data

GRI and SASB have had a remarkable impact on this field. However, they are only two out of several organizations that provide additional clarity to better understand sustainability data and its applications. Here are some of the other key players:

- CDP, The Carbon Disclosure Project - Started in 2002, it initially focused on climate-related issues but now includes water, supply chain, and forests related topics.

- SDGs, The Sustainable Development Goals of the United Nations - A collection of 17 interlinked objectives including poverty, hunger, education, and equality designed to serve as a "shared blueprint for peace and prosperity for people and the planet, now and into the future."

- GRESB, The Global Real Estate Sustainability Benchmark - An organization that provides actionable and transparent ESG data to financial markets. Their initial focus was on infrastructure and real estate.

- UNPRI, UN Principles for Responsible Investment - Developed for investors by investors, it intends to support its international network of investor signatories in incorporating environmental, social, and governance (ESG) factors into their investment and ownership decisions.

From ESG Indexes to ETFs: The Evolution of Sustainable Investing

Ratings and scores allow for an easy comparison of companies and their ESG performance. It is now common to use this information to create benchmarks and indexes that show how a company or industry is doing in relation to ESG. The first ESG index, the Domini 400 Social Index, was created in 1990 by KLD Research & Analytics. Today, there are over 1,000 ESG indexes available, reflecting the increasing interest from investors in sustainable products and the need for measurement tools to evaluate them. These indexes have led to the creation of ESG mutual funds and exchange-traded funds (ETFs) that can be invested in. In 2022, the growth of these products rose by 53% to $2.7 trillion. There are now ESG products available to suit every definition of sustainability.

In the social aspect, there is a growing number of DEI (Diversity, Equity, and Inclusion) funds that have their investment philosophy focused on supporting companies with robust corporate diversity policies. These investments are geared towards organizations led by black,

Indigenous, people of color, LGBTQ+, immigrant, neurodiverse, and/or disability community members. Examples of these types of funds include The Adasina Social Justice All Cap Global ETF (ticker: JSTC) which is based on the Adasina Social Justice Index and The Impact Shares NAACP Minority Empowerment ETF (ticker: NACP) which is based on the Morningstar Minority Empowerment TR USD.

There are also a number of funds on the environmental side, focusing on clean (carbon-free) energy. These funds invest in companies that have a low fossil fuel exposure and carbon footprint. This automatically excludes fossil fuel-based companies such as coal, oil, and gas producers, and coal-fired utilities. One example of these types of funds is the iShares Global Clean Energy ETF (ticker: ICLN). These funds can also be very specific in terms of the type of clean energy they invest in. For instance, if an investor wants to support the growth of solar energy, they can consider the Invesco Solar ETF (ticker: TAN), or for wind-based energy investment there is the First Trust Global Wind Energy ETF (ticker: FAN). With these options, it's easy to align your investments with your values and support the transition to a cleaner energy future.

Investors now have many options to align their investments with their values. For example, if they want to combine their social and environmental values, they can consider the TIAA-CREF Social Choice Low Carbon Equity Fund (ticker: TNWCX). This fund aims to achieve a favorable long-term return by investing in the overall U.S. stock market, with a focus on companies that meet certain environmental, social, and governance criteria, including criteria related to carbon emissions and fossil fuel reserves. Another example is the ETFB Green SRI REITs ETF (ticker: RITA), which is a real estate investment with a high ESG score and is also compliant with the social values of the Islamic faith. These are just a few examples of the many investment alternatives that are becoming available to investors every day.

The Growth of Non-Traditional (Alternative) ESG Investing

Going beyond retail products like indexes, mutual funds, and ETFs, there has been significant growth in non-traditional investments in the managed funds industry. Venture Capital and Private Equity firms are not only creating specialized ESG funds for their investors, but they are also incorporating specific ESG considerations into their due diligence process when evaluating potential investments. They look for private companies that adopt good ESG practices from the outset, as these companies are likely to be in a better position to provide any ESG-specific representations and warranties required by future investors and to defend against price adjustments due to negative ESG factors.

Even the hedge fund industry is getting in on the trend, with several hedge funds applying to become signatories of the United Nations Principles for Responsible Investing (UN PRI) and creating ESG versions of their flagship products for investors to consider. This has prompted the UN PRI to offer "The Responsible Investment Due Diligence Questionnaire for Hedge Funds" on their website. Signatories of the UN PRI publicly commit to adopt and implement the principles, where consistent with their fiduciary responsibilities, and to evaluate and improve the content of the principles over time. This commitment aligns their investment activities with the broader interests of society and improves their ability to meet their commitments to beneficiaries.

ESG Derivatives: Unlocking Capital for Sustainable Investments

The evolution of ESG investing has led to the creation of a wide range of financial products that cater to different types of investors. These products range from passive indexes to actively managed ESG portfolios and even highly sophisticated financially engineered derivatives. Derivatives can play an important role in ESG investing by enabling more capital to be channeled towards sustainable investments, helping market participants to hedge risk related to ESG factors, facilitating transparency, price discovery, and market efficiency, and contributing to long-termism.

One example of these derivatives is ESG-related credit derivatives, which are designed to encourage more capital to be invested in renewable energy projects. Examples include Power Purchase Agreements (PPAs), Renewable Energy Certificate

(REC) futures, wind index futures, and low carbon fuel standard futures.

Sustainability-linked derivatives are another example, which is designed to create an environmental, social and governance-linked cash flow that is a component of, or relates to, a conventional derivatives instrument. This is achieved by using previously defined key performance indicators (KPIs) to monitor compliance with stated ESG targets. These derivatives can provide investors with innovative ways to invest in sustainable projects while also aligning their investments with their values and priorities.

Software Market Booms: Innovative Solutions for ESG

The software industry is booming with innovative solutions to support the entire ESG data lifecycle. From data collection and organization for companies to portfolio and risk management tools for investment professionals, and even mobile apps for individual consumers, the ESG software market is rapidly expanding. With an estimated growth rate of 28% per year, it's projected to surpass $1.5 billion dollars by the mid-2020s.

There are now a variety of software options available to help manage and measure ESG exposures and risks. These tools include features such as data collection, analysis, and reporting, as well as scorecards and dashboards to provide a clear view of an organization's progress toward ESG goals. Leading enterprise resource planning (ERP) software companies like SAP, Oracle, and Sage Software have already integrated ESG capabilities into their inventory, human resources, and financial suites. Additionally, a growing number of specialist software companies have emerged, with the inaugural ESG Tech 100 listing including 15 companies that specialize in corporate sustainability data management. Many of these companies are young, with most being under five years old and having less than 10 employees. Companies like Key ESG Metrio and Dcycle are prime examples of software that were specifically designed to help organizations implement a reporting framework, automate data collection, measure ESG performance in real time, and manage the outbound delivery of ESG messaging and data.

Context Labs (profiled at the end of this chapter) delivers these capabilities on a blockchain-enabled platform solution which includes secure distributed ledgers, network graph analytics, and data interoperability and visualization for publishing, financial, trading, and supply chain data.

It's important for companies not only to understand their own ESG performance and risks but also to know how the companies they work with are performing. To address this, organizations like Shared Assessments focus on helping companies build successful and resilient partnerships with third parties. They also work with leading supply chain software companies such as Archer, Sentio, and Supply Wisdom to incorporate ESG capabilities into their products.

In addition, the ESG investment community is being introduced to new software tools as well. Investors who need tools for portfolio reporting, investment screening, workflow integration, and deep-dive research are turning to start-ups like Clarity.AI, Yves Blue, and GaiaLens. These companies are "Solutions Providers" and offer a combination of third-party research and data with their own. Some use artificial intelligence and advanced technologies, while others focus on emerging regulatory reporting requirements. But all of these companies pay close attention to the user experience and provide easy-to-use solutions that are intuitive and easy to understand.

ESG regulations are being introduced globally, leading to the quick development and release of software to support compliance and reporting. These regulations include those in Europe for TCFD, SFDR, and EU-Taxonomy, in the US where the SEC is implementing Climate-Disclosure rules, in Australia where the government is providing guidance on Greenwashing, and in Singapore where guidelines for Sovereign Green Bonds are being developed. This software assists investors in understanding the regulatory impact on their portfolios, submitting required data and reports to regulators, and informing end investors of their regulatory obligations. Some prominent providers of ESG compliance software include Confluence Software, ACA, and LaMeer Inc.

Universities Embrace ESG

The CFA Certification has always been a benchmark for me. In the mid-1980s, as I entered the financial services industry, ethics was a crucial issue due to the "junk bond" corruption on Wall Street. As a result, ethics became a prominent topic on the CFA exam. In recent years, two new topics on the exam have been ESG and Blockchain. The CFA Institute consistently monitors key debates and evolving issues in the investment industry. ESG investing and analysis have become increasingly relevant to investment professionals globally as governments, asset owners, and high-net-worth investors consider the impact of ESG factors on their investments and local markets. They believe that a more thorough examination of ESG factors by financial professionals can improve the fundamental analysis they undertake and ultimately the investment choices they make. The CFA Institute is particularly focused on the quality and comparability of the ESG information provided by corporate issuers and how to integrate various ESG factors into the investment selection process. To the best of my knowledge, the CFA exam does not remove topics, which tells me that ESG is here to stay and has become very important to the investment industry. You would be hard-pressed today to find any university, college, or even community college that doesn't offer a course in some ESG-related topic. Look at this list of undergraduate and graduate degrees available:

- Certificate in Sustainability
- Masters in Environment and Business (MEB)
- Masters in Environment and Sustainability (MES)
- Certificate in Renewable Energy
- Master of Science in Sustainability, Water Resource Management, Community-based sustainability
- Certificate, Energy Policy and Climate
- Certified Expert in Climate & Renewable Energy
- Sustainable Investing Professional
- MBA in Renewables, Strategic Leadership towards Sustainability, Sustainable Residential Design, Green Economics.

Jobs, Jobs, and More Jobs

Deloitte plans to create over 100,000 new jobs in the next five years, many focused-on climate change and sustainability. Not only is ESG becoming a popular career choice, but it is also one of the most pronounced industry trends in recent times that has the potential to impact a much wider range of careers within the financial sector. From analysts in the investor relations department to Chief Sustainability Officers reporting to the board. Here are some popular roles:

- Director of Sustainability
- Environmental policy manager
- Director of environment, energy, & safety
- Director of social & environmental responsibility
- Chief officer of environment
- Social & environmental sustainability manager
- Chief of environmental health and safety
- Certified sustainability administrator

Sustainable Investing: ESG Consultants Lead the Way

ESG consultants have in-depth knowledge about ESG strategy, program implementation and reporting. They can provide clarity and insights into the risks and opportunities associated with addressing environmental, social, and governance issues. Many major consulting firms, such as EY, KPMG, Deloitte, McKinsey, and Boston Consulting Group, offer ESG and sustainability services, which may include decarbonization, reporting, sustainable finance, and DEI (diversity, equity, and inclusion) engagements. As demand for assurance in ESG disclosures increases, the need for audit and assurance services that provide an independent review of voluntarily reported information also rises.

Some notable specialist firms have emerged, such as Agendi, which helps companies transition to a low-carbon economy in a positive manner, and the Governance and Accountability Institute (G&I Institute). G&I Institute works with both companies and investors to help them understand the "new norms" of corporate sustainability, corporate responsibility, corporate citizenship, and ESG strategies and performance, as well as the growing acceptance of sustainable investing, ESG investing, socially responsible investing, and impact investing.

ESG Conferences: A Wealth of Opportunities

There are currently more than one hundred ESG and SRI conferences held annually. When you add in the ESG tracks of non-ESG conferences, university symposiums, and vendor events, the number of events quickly rises to the hundreds. Some well-known conferences in the sustainability and ESG field include Responsible Investor (RI), Bloomberg, Refinitiv, and the Sustainable Investment Forum (SIF). The longest-running conference is "ESG for Impact," which has been consistently offered by First Affirmative Financial Network for over 30 years.

Multimedia to Keep Yourself Informed and Learning

The Amazon Bookstore tells us that there are over 6,000 titles available that refer to ESG. As of the day of its publishing, this book is the only one that I know of that is focused specifically on ESG Data and the businesses around it. I'm sure that there will be more to come. On Amazon alone, over 200 books about ESG were published in the past three months,

70 if you count only last month with more than 38 titles coming soon. Outside the book printing and ebook world, there are hundreds of websites, dozens of daily newsletters, and as many podcasts available for your listening pleasure.

As this chapter has shown, the evolution of ESG data has opened up a vast array of business and investment opportunities. From negative screening to researching ESG risk factors to creating new financial products, software, and services, the possibilities are endless. The number of businesses related to ESG data is projected to surpass one thousand by 2025, making this an exciting and rapidly evolving field. Through highlighting some of the most innovative and impactful players in the field, I hope I have brought unique insights that will help you in your journey through the ESG world.

A Real World Example

 Context Labs

Topic: The Business of ESG Data
To: Mike Poisson
Fm: Mark McDivitt – COO of Context Labs, BV

Questions

- *What was the problem you saw?*
- *What was the solution that Context Labs came up with?*
- *How is this going to change the Business of ESG data moving forward?*

The Problem – *Trust in Data*

During my tenure at State Street Corporation as Global Head of ESG, the ESG team built and deployed a decision support tool called ESGX™ to assist its clients in quantifying the non-traditional financial risks embedded in the $34+ trillion global custody portfolios. The feedback received was always the same, effectively, how do we:

- Trust the data?
- Interpret the subjective, qualitative nature of the ESG scores in measuring risk?
- Manage the low correlation between the ESG data vendors' ratings on the same portfolio of assets?

The Solution – *Context Labs Data Fabric Immutably™ Platform*

While researching the universe of third-party ESG data vendors in an effort to tackle these problems, I met Dan Harple, Founder and CEO of Context Labs. After listening to Dan's vision and approach to addressing global challenges like climate change by transforming complex data into measurable results, I was convinced that I had finally found the solution that I was looking for. I made the decision to leave my career of 10+ years at State Street Corporation with 40,000+ employees to join this start-up of 17 people at the time and get on with tackling the central challenge facing the Business of ESG Data today – the ability to trust the data.

Context Labs is a software company headquartered in Cambridge, MA that turns complex data into measurable results through its tech stack called Immutably™. By leveraging AI and Machine Learning in capturing multiple sources of disparate data, Context Labs is able to deliver in real time empirical facts that lead to trusted insights – the key component that is lacking with traditional ESG measurement approaches today. Built on an open API architecture, Context Labs' blockchain-enabled data fabric platform allows organizations to continuously ingest, encrypt, and contextualize data from any source at scale, connect the dots in an increasingly fragmented ecosystem, and make data an accelerant for global change. It's critical to note that blockchain is not some magic wand. 'Garbage' data dropped into the blockchain will still deliver 'garbage' results. Context Labs mitigates this risk by first deconstructing, reconstructing and then 'shrink wrapping' the data, effectively stripping out any of the outlier data points, then dropping the data onto its private, distributed ledger. The end result is an empirically trusted, quantifiable measurement of a targeted asset that can then be optimally managed.

The Impact – Quantitative, *Empirical Facts becoming the Standard over Qualitative Scores, Ratings, and Estimates within the Business of ESG Data*

The business of ESG data to date, in this case the 'E' of ESG, scores, ratings, and estimates has not been effective in delivering the level of empirical truth needed by institutional investors to be able to make better-informed decisions and subsequently make larger asset allocation commitments targeted at climate change. Context Labs breaks this bottleneck by supporting global entities in quantifying the environmental externalities embedded in portfolio company holdings, which in turn is moving the bar on what is now expected from the business of ESG data. The net impact is an acceleration of the energy transition and ideally a look back in a decade to suggest that the business of ESG data 2.0, in fact, has succeeded in slowing down global warming to under 1.5 degrees C.

Chapter 6

TEN INDUSTRY OBSERVATIONS

The changes in attitude and responsibility that ESG promoted for the past decades is a one-way path to a better future. There is no going back from here. We're not going to wake up tomorrow morning and decide to pollute. We're not going to turn on the news and hear "You know what? That whole women's rights thing... it's a bunch of nonsense". And even those voices of "Drill, baby Drill" are becoming quieter. For the most part, the world acknowledges that there are environmental issues that need addressing. The world is getting hotter. We need alternatives to fossil fuels. There is a limit to our natural resources.

There are also social issues that need our attention. Hunger and poverty and homelessness still exist. And, again, as my friend begins all of her keynote speeches, *"Without the G (Governance), why bother?"* With all this, the business of ESG Data will continue to grow for decades to come.

Here are some thoughts, possibilities, and predictions that I have for the ESG Data industry in the next few years.

1 - In the short term, regulators will drive the ESG Research Data efforts.

ESG research and data have been around for some time. It has evolved from business involvement (guns, alcohol, tobacco, South Africa) to individual E, S, and G factors (polluters, water abusers, women on boards) to very specific quantifiable data (metric tons of carbon emissions). As a result, there are over 150 ESG data providers serving this industry collectively offering thousands of ESG data observations. How will this change? With the introduction of numerous regulations around the globe, the regulators are telling the world what they feel is the most important ESG data (today). For SFDR.... For EU Taxonomy... For the SEC Disclosure

Proposal... The regulators are asking for very specific quantitative data on carbon, waste, and water. They are looking for evidence of companies "doing no significant harm".

Researchers need to figure this out or they will be left behind. There is a whole new market to serve. Whereas traditionally research companies were catering to consumers that were knowledgeable in ESG, the current opportunity is with "boxer tickers". Those who don't necessarily care about ESG, sustainability, and the cause but who are required to comply in order to stay in business or avoid fines and other penalties. This regulatory data also requires a special type of research since what is being asked for isn't typically volunteered or easily reportable. The research firms are rapidly developing sophisticated estimation models that incorporate artificial intelligence and other modern tools to combine with traditional data that companies have begun to offer.

2 - In the long term, ESG data will become more sophisticated and more specific.

As we enter the Regulatory and Compliance Age of ESG we will see a whole new roster of players enter the game. Many reluctantly. A number of them preferred to sit on the sidelines because sustainability and ESG weren't important to them or because while there was lots of evidence that ESG *may* affect financial performance, there's no universally accepted and undisputed proof that ESG *did* contribute to positive returns.

Now that their participation is mandatory, and they must address ESG for compliance and reporting, they'll need to acquire ESG data. With no prior knowledge of where to get this data, they will initially rely on large name-brand vendors without questioning the high expense. But eventually, they will look more closely at the data. In trying to understand it, they will question, critique, analyze, evaluate, and elevate what the data is and the quality of the data. They will eventually look to the broader market of data vendors as their imaginations evolve.

I see this as an exercise in Massively Parallel Processing (MPP) where we are about to unleash thousands of sophisticated financial investing minds on finding returns and generating Alpha from ESG data and using ESG as a competitive tool to differentiate themselves in their investing, product positioning, and marketing. They will be demanding NEW data the likes of which we've never considered. Who knows, we might learn that the most significant performance factor is to invest in companies that have caused the least amount of harm to salmon.

3 - The quality of the data is on a one-way trip to improvement

Since I've been in the ESG Research and Data field, I've attended hundreds of conferences, seminars, webinars, and symposiums where ESG data was discussed. For the most part, these sessions were attacks on the research and data companies – they all focused on "what was wrong" with the data. I have to tell you, I walked out of many of these sessions really questioning the field that I had chosen. But invariably, somebody would always put their arm around me and assure me that whatever the state of the ESG research business was in, it was still vital, necessary, and important. It just has its problems.

Now that the industry is getting some focus (with the regulators), a "new" discussion about data quality can happen. There will be more eyes on the ball. New reporting standards will be developed. Companies reporting ESG data will hire third-party consultants to audit and review their submissions. Assurance firms will attest that investment companies are following their own advertised approaches.

There is unlimited opportunity for small, medium and large sized service providers to offer reporting, consulting, audit, and assurance services to every member of the ESG lifecycle – framework provider, reporting entity, investment company, investor, regulator, and so on.

4 - Insurance makes its entrance to the ESG folder

With the increase in demand for ESG transparency as a result of regulation it's just a matter of time before insurance products will have to adapt. Shareholders and interest groups are scrutinizing ESG policies and disclosures. Lawsuits are arising that include claims of fraud, breaches of fiduciary duties and violations of securities fraud. Companies' sustainable investments and commitments have the potential to reshape their risk profiles in D&O, E&O, and EPL, among other areas.

Underwriting is rapidly evolving to focus on the emerging risks and opportunities. As insurers, brokers and agents, and risk managers work together to fully understand companies' ESG-related planning process, there will be a sharp focus on company risk disclosures as well as progress toward ESG targets as represented to regulators, investors, and employees.

5 - ESG Solutions Providers and their new version of the Space Race.

According to the Governance & Accountability Institute's 2022 "Sustainability Reporting In Focus" Report, 96% of the S&P 500 companies and 81% of the Russell 1000 companies have issued a sustainability report. That's pretty good progress and participation until you look at Dun and Bradstreet's global commercial database which contains more than 225 million business records in 200 countries.

Investors and solutions providers both recognize that the firm that creates and delivers a solution that can be universally adopted and implemented by the masses will own the ESG solutions industry. There is no lack of participants in this race. Existing software and services companies serving the Private Equity markets are working on this challenge as are start-up software companies, banks of all sizes, international exchanges and consulting firms.

It's not a matter of "if" a private company would benefit from such a service but "when." Private companies' cost of capital is already impacted by their ESG performance. Private investors are taking ESG factors into their investment analysis. And private companies are seeing the effect that high ESG performance is having on their sales and marketing. We're not yet at the stage where consumers are as motivated by an ESG score as they are with the published calorie count on the menu before they make their selection. But that day may not be that far away.

6 - M&A in the ESG solutions and data space continues to grow

In the past couple of years, we've seen several transactions where large ESG research companies acquired independent ESG data specialists. Morningstar acquired all of Sustainalytics after making a minority investment years earlier. S&P has acquired several companies including RobecoSAM, Trucost, and The Climate Service. ESG analytics companies Metrio and Envizi were acquired by NASDAQ and IBM respectively.

Since this is a very "data-intensive" industry, it may be attractive to "own" the source of data that feeds all of these solutions. Research and data companies seem to be acquiring other data companies while consulting and services companies seem to be acquiring analytics providers. We've not seen an investment that looks to offer a full cycle vertical solution of data, analytics reporting, and compliance, at least, not yet. Venture Capital and Private Equity investors are actively looking to add high-quality ESG data and service companies to their portfolios.

7 - Profits from unintended consequences.

A few years ago, I met a leading ETF researcher and industry expert. I wanted to engage him in a discussion about ESG, sustainable investing, and social responsibility but he really had no interest in the topic or the discussion. In 2022 with global equity markets getting crushed, this same industry leader wrote an article that I found fascinating. He was promoting ESG as an investment strategy. Let me be clear, his views on ESG probably haven't changed a bit since we first met, however, he had developed a use for ESG – as a tool for Tax Loss Harvesting. Since so much money was invested and lost in equities and equity index products, he suggests that investors sell their investments and re-invest into the ESG versions of the same index or product. This strategy should elude the wash-sale rule while allowing the investor to participate in the rebound of the same or similar equities. If a significant amount of capital followed this one simple strategy and then we were able to draw positive mathematical correlations and conclusions about the performance of ESG investments, the floodgates of ESG investing would be opened.

8 - Everything will have an ESG lens.

When I first began my career in the ESG data industry, I focused on companies that reported ESG data and the investors who invested in them. However, I have since learned that there are many different applications of ESG data and that it can have an impact on every aspect of business.

One example is the way that ESG data is affecting the supply chain and the third-party risk management industry. Companies are now being asked to report on their emissions, which are divided into three categories: Scope 1 (direct emissions from owned or controlled sources), Scope 2 (indirect emissions from purchased electricity, steam, heating and cooling), and Scope 3 (all other indirect emissions in the company's value chain). This is a major challenge for companies, and third-party risk solutions providers are adapting their products and services to meet this new requirement.

Another example is the impact of ESG on taxation and transfer pricing. Transfer pricing is a technique used by multinational corporations to shift profits to tax havens. I was recently asked to help form a working group to study the impact of ESG on this technique. At first, I couldn't see how ESG data would be relevant to the topic, but after discussing with my network industry experts, I learned that there are many risks and exposures related to social and governance issues that are affecting and being affected by tax and transfer pricing.

9 - If you're Greenwashing and you know it, clap your hands.

Greenwashing is a term used to describe companies making false or misleading claims about their environmental practices. It is often used to attract environmentally conscious consumers, but can also be found in other industries, such as financial software, where companies may make claims about their ESG (Environmental, Social, and Governance) capabilities without being able to back them up with substance. The SEC has recently begun to address this issue by targeting fund managers who profit from exaggerated ESG claims, but this does not address all the other businesses making false claims. Buyers beware of these false claims and sellers be prepared to be called out on your ESG and sustainability statements.

10 - The many languages of ESG – is it Greek to you?

A significant barrier to advancement in the sustainability and ESG "cause" is the inherent confusion and lack of clarity in the messaging. It's a field that is discussed and referred to by many terms including ESG, SRI, CSR, IMPACT, and Green. Its regulations are equally confusing with SFDR, EU Taxonomy, TCFD, and the proposed SEC Greenwashing Rule. Reporting standards include SASB (now IFRS), GRI, CDP, CDSB, and IIRC. And the United Nations is promoting its PRI, SDGs, and GCPs.

This alphabet soup has failed to create a consensus and a singularity of focus. Maybe that's just too much to ask. There does seem to be a consensus amongst those outside of the ESG world who simply refer to those involved as "tree huggers", lefties and socialists. They need hard facts, statistical correlations to claimed results, and indisputable positive returns before they will join the game.

I've converted some of these tough customers through the use of academic papers that use Discounted Cash Flow (DCF) analysis and Cost of Capital analysis to describe successful and impactful ESG initiatives. These initiatives link ESG to cash flow in five important ways:

1. Facilitating top-line growth,
2. Reducing costs,
3. Minimizing regulatory and legal interventions,
4. Increasing employee productivity
5. Optimizing investment and capital expenditures.

I broke through to this accused non-believer in sustainability. It was a kind of secret decoder ring that they needed to make the leap into accepting ESG. I believe that this language needs to be further developed.

The shift towards a more responsible and sustainable approach to business, promoted by ESG is here to stay. It is a key component to imagining a better future. The business of ESG data will continue to grow in the coming decades as more companies and investors recognize the importance of this information in making responsible and sustainable decisions. It is not only a moral imperative but also a smart business strategy.

Chapter 7

THE NEXT STEP

When I first entered the ESG Data business I spent a lot of time at conferences, symposiums, seminars, and other events. Typically, there was a session on ESG Data where all of the problems with ESG data were discussed: It's inconsistent, there were no standards, the companies reporting weren't transparent, the vendors selling the data weren't transparent, and the data was just wrong, irrelevant, and not helpful. I must say that after a few of these sessions, I really questioned my chosen career. Invariably someone would come up to me, put their arm around me, and comfort me with the importance of what we were doing and that the debate will only improve the quality and importance of the research and data.

At these conferences, it was common to end the day by asking the final speaker about their vision for ESG-specific conferences in the future. The frequent response seemed to be that there will be no need for such conferences because ESG will be so fully integrated into everyday business practices and life. While the industry is growing and progress is being made, it may take longer than ten years for this integration to occur. Additionally, progress is also being made in the field of ESG data, which is becoming increasingly important in evaluating the environmental and social impact of a company or organization.

The field of sustainability is vast and complex, and there is no one-size-fits-all approach to evaluating the environmental and social impact of a company or organization. However, with the increasing importance of ESG data, it is crucial that efforts be made to standardize and improve the ways in which we measure and report on ESG performance. This will not only help companies and organizations make better decisions but will also lead to a more sustainable future for all of us. Over time, we hope that a consistent application of these measures will lead to an improvement in our ability to do well and do good simultaneously.

Regarding ESG Data:

- If you or your business has a need for ESG Data to support your investment activities, fulfill your investors' mandates, and comply with international regulations or standards, please contact me at IdealRatings.

- If you are interested in starting a business that requires ESG data, also contact me at IdealRatings.

You can reach me directly at mpoisson@idealrating.com. You can also learn more about IdealRatings by going to: https://www.idealratings.com/

Regarding this Book and Anything Else:

If you need help understanding ESG Data, if you have an ESG story to share, or if you are thinking

about starting an ESG Solutions business, feel free to contact me at:
Michael@theesgdatarevolution.com or
+1.201.462.7500

Finally, I'm a firm believer that you are uniquely qualified to be working with certain people - not everybody but people who "get" you and what you and your business stand for. I feel the same about my business, and in order for us to see if we are a good fit, I'd like to take a moment now to share a bit more about myself and my background.

To that end, I had my publisher, Paul McManus, interview me so you can get to know me better and make a judgment for yourself to see if you think I might be the right person to help you.

Watch the video at
www.theesgdatarevoltion.com/video
The recorded video is 21 minutes long.

I look forward to hearing from you, and more importantly, working together to help you create new opportunities from the ESG Data Revolution!

RESOURCES

www.theesgdatarevoltion.com

https://www.idealratings.com/

https://www.linkedin.com/in/michaelpoisson/

ABOUT THE AUTHOR

Michael Poisson has spent his entire career building growing and successfully exiting a number of FINTECH companies. His passion for Corporate Responsibility and ESG Data began when he joined IdealRatings to expand the reach of its research and data into new markets. He is currently a Managing Director responsible for IdealRatings' North American business development based in New York.

He has previously held senior executive positions at Investor Analytics (now Confluence Software), a Risk Transparency Service for asset managers and asset owners, Cogency Software (now Backstop Solutions Group) a provider of technology solutions to the hedge fund industry and SunGard Treasury Systems (now FIS), a supplier of internet and intranet treasury and risk management solutions.

Mr. Poisson is a graduate from Rensselaer Polytechnic Institute where he received a B.S. in Management and was a goaltender for the NCAA Division, I Champion RPI Engineers hockey team.

Printed in Great Britain
by Amazon

27272071R00066